The Magic School B

Inside the Human Body

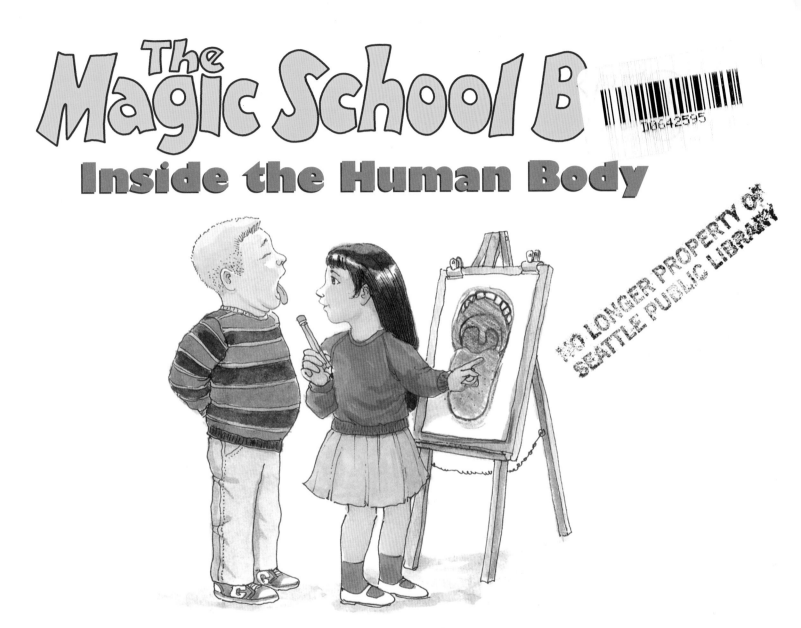

By Joanna Cole / Illustrated by Bruce Degen

Scholastic Inc.
New York • Toronto • London • Auckland
Sydney • Mexico City • New Delhi • Hong Kong

The author and illustrator wish to thank Dr. Arnold J. Capute,
Associate Professor of Pediatrics, Director, Division of Child Development,
Johns Hopkins University School of Medicine, for his help in preparing this book.

ISBN 978-0-545-28947-4

Text copyright © 1989 by Joanna Cole
Illustrations copyright © 1989 by Bruce Degen
All rights reserved. Published by Scholastic Inc.

SCHOLASTIC, THE MAGIC SCHOOL BUS, and associated logos are trademarks and/or registered trademarks of Scholastic Inc.

19 18 17 16 15 14 13 12   18 19 20 21/0

Printed in China   95
This edition first printing, January 2011

The illustrator used pen and ink, watercolor, color pencil, and gouache for the paintings in this book.

WE'RE GOING TO LEARN ABOUT OURSELVES. THIS SHOULD INTEREST YOU, ARNOLD!

It all began when Ms. Frizzle
showed our class a filmstrip
about the human body.
We knew trouble was about to start,
because we knew Ms. Frizzle
was the strangest teacher in the school

MY FAVORITE HERBIVORE

MY FAVORITE CARNIVORE

I CAN'T TAKE THE PRESSURE!

MY FAVORIT OMNIVORE

4

5

YOUR BODY IS MADE OF CELLS
by Rachel

Your body seems to be all one piece, but actually it is made of trillions of tiny pieces, called cells.

MY BODY IS MADE OF TRILLIONS OF CELLS.

SO IS MINE!

The very next day, The Friz made us do an experiment on our own bodies.

SEE YOUR OWN CELLS

Most cells are so small that we can't see them without a microscope.

① Gently scrape inside of cheek with toothpick

② Stir end of toothpick in drop of water on a slide.

③ Add a drop of Iodine Solution to color cells.

④ Look at slide under microscope. See your cells.

OOOH, WEIRD!

Then she announced that we were going on a class trip to the science museum. We were going to see an exhibit about how our bodies get energy from the food we eat.

YOUR CELLS NEED ENERGY TO HELP YOU GROW, MOVE, TALK, THINK, AND PLAY.

Jail cell

JUST BEING IN MS. FRIZZLE'S CLASS TAKES ALL MY ENERGY.

DIFFERENT KINDS OF CELLS HAVE DIFFERENT JOBS
by Gregory

Lung cells help you breathe

ODE TO JELLY

Muscle cells help you move

Brain Cells help you think.

YOUR MOUTH HAS THOUSANDS OF TASTE BUDS!
by Arnold

Different parts of the mouth have taste buds that are best at detecting different flavors.

New research shows that the taste buds are arranged like this:

BITTER
SOUR
SALT
SWEET

DID YOU KNOW?
The middle of your tongue has <u>no</u> taste buds!

The trip started out like any other trip.
We rode to the museum
in the old school bus.
Along the way,
we stopped at a park for lunch.

LEFT OVER FISH STICKS?! ICK!

I'LL TRADE YOU THESE TERRIFIC FISH STICKS FOR THAT HORRIBLE PEANUT BUTTER AND BANANA SANDWICH.

FORGET IT!

TAKE A LOOK AT HER SHOES.

PLEASE! I'M EATING!

When it was time to go,
everyone got back on the bus—
everyone but Arnold.
He was still at the picnic table,
daydreaming and eating
a bag of Cheesie-Weesies.

> WHEN YOU EAT, YOUR BODY DIGESTS THE FOOD SO YOUR CELLS CAN USE IT TO MAKE ENERGY.

YOUR BODY NEEDS GOOD FOOD
by Carmen

For high energy and good growing power, eat lots and lots of:

CEREAL BROWN RICE

whole grain bread, cereal, and pasta

fresh fruits and vegetables

Eat a smaller amount of:

YOGURT

Milk and milk products

meat, poultry, egg, fish and fats

AND NOT TOO MUCH JUNK FOOD!!!

A SCIENCE WORD
by Dorothy Ann

Digestion comes from a word that means to divide. When food is digested it is divided into smaller and smaller parts.

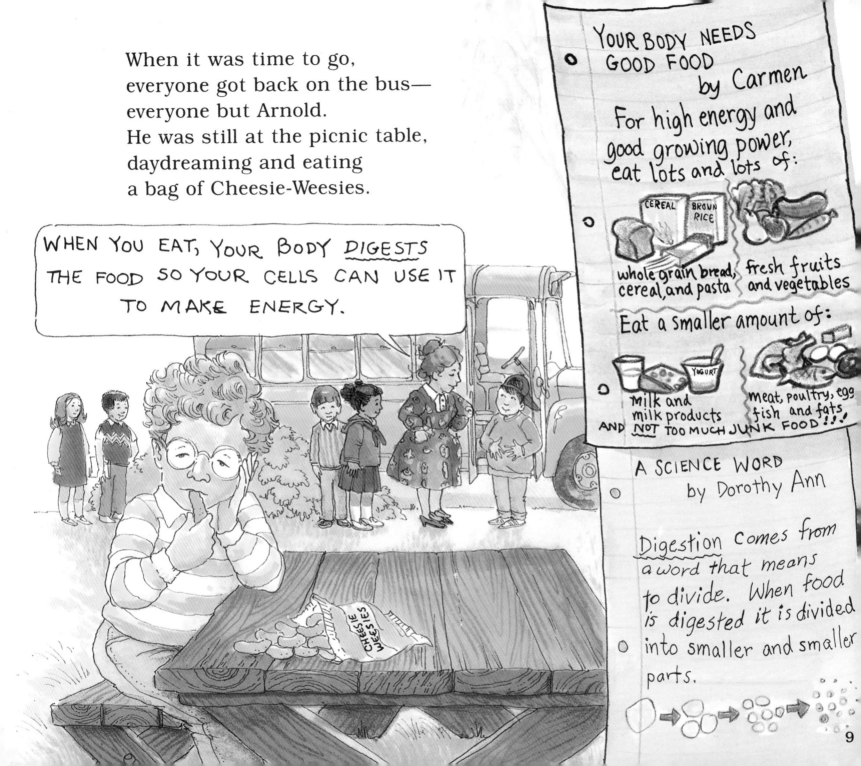

9

"Hurry up, Arnold!" called Ms. Frizzle. She reached for the ignition key, but instead she pushed a strange little button nearby.

ARNOLD'S REALLY OUT TO LUNCH.

At once, we started shrinking and spinning through the air.

From inside, we couldn't see what was happening. All we knew was that we landed suddenly...

GULP! HEY, WHERE'S THE BUS?

and then we were going down a dark tunnel.
We had no idea where we were.
But, as usual, Ms. Frizzle knew.
She said we were inside a human body,
going down the esophagus—
the tube that leads from the mouth
to the stomach.
Most of us were too upset
about leaving Arnold behind
to pay much attention.

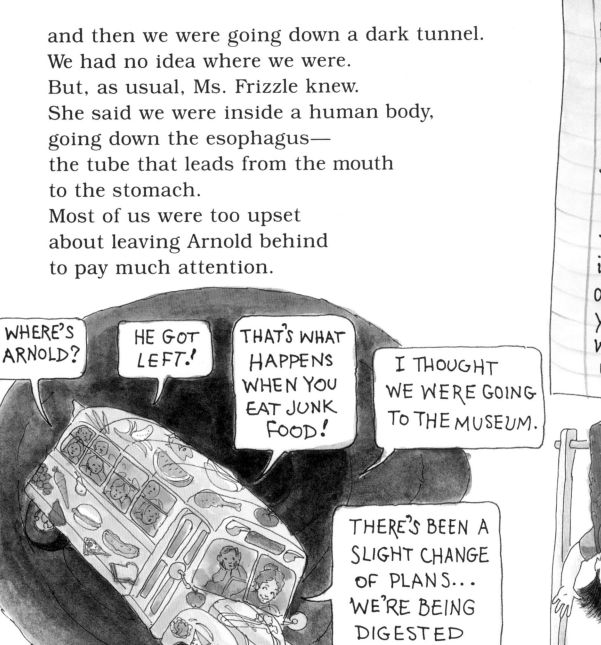

WHERE'S ARNOLD?

HE GOT LEFT!

THAT'S WHAT HAPPENS WHEN YOU EAT JUNK FOOD!

I THOUGHT WE WERE GOING TO THE MUSEUM.

THERE'S BEEN A SLIGHT CHANGE OF PLANS... WE'RE BEING DIGESTED INSTEAD.

FOOD GOES TO YOUR STOMACH THROUGH THE ESOPHAGUS
by Wanda

The food does not just fall down. It is pushed along by muscle actions the way toothpaste is squeezed out of a tube. That's why you can swallow even when you are upside down.

MUSCLES SQUEEZE TO PUSH FOOD TO YOUR STOMACH

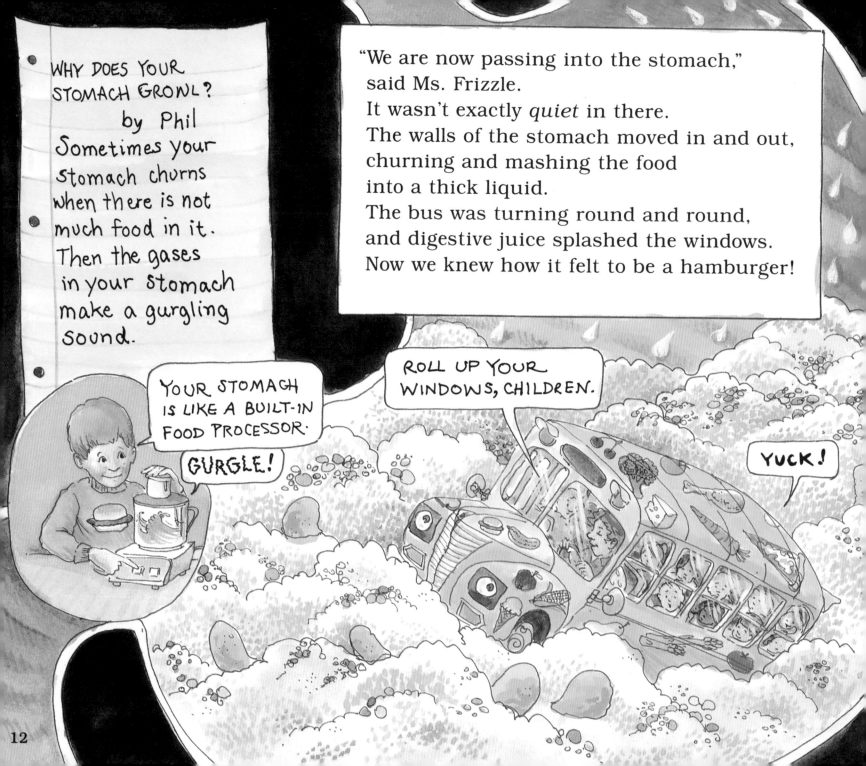

WHY DOES YOUR STOMACH GROWL?
by Phil

Sometimes your stomach churns when there is not much food in it. Then the gases in your stomach make a gurgling sound.

"We are now passing into the stomach," said Ms. Frizzle.
It wasn't exactly *quiet* in there.
The walls of the stomach moved in and out, churning and mashing the food into a thick liquid.
The bus was turning round and round, and digestive juice splashed the windows.
Now we knew how it felt to be a hamburger!

YOUR STOMACH IS LIKE A BUILT-IN FOOD PROCESSOR.

GURGLE!

ROLL UP YOUR WINDOWS, CHILDREN.

YUCK!

WHY ARE THE INTESTINES COILED UP?
by John

In an adult the intestines are 7.5 meters (25 feet) long. If they were stretched out straight, a person would have to be as tall as a house.

STOMACH

FOOD GOES FROM THE STOMACH TO THE SMALL INTESTINE

WASTE GOES OUT THROUGH THE LARGE INTESTINE

The small intestine was a coiled-up hollow tube.
The inner walls of the tube were covered with tiny "fingers" called *villi*.
"In the *villi* are tiny blood vessels. Food molecules are taken into these blood vessels," said Ms. Frizzle.
"Once the food is in the blood, it can travel all over the body."

We felt ourselves getting even smaller, and Ms. Frizzle started driving into one of the *villi*.
She was going straight into a blood vessel!

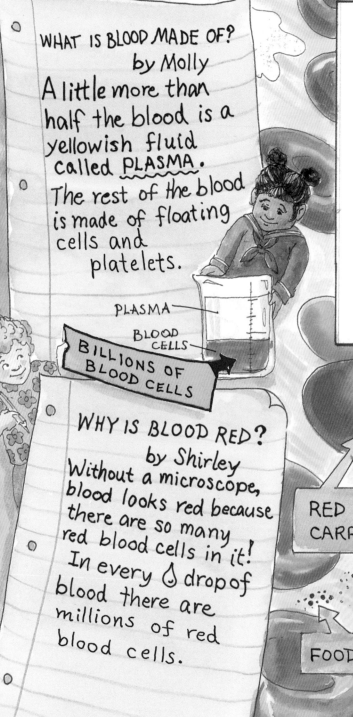

WHAT IS BLOOD MADE OF?
by Molly
A little more than half the blood is a yellowish fluid called PLASMA.
The rest of the blood is made of floating cells and platelets.

PLASMA
BLOOD CELLS

BILLIONS OF BLOOD CELLS

WHY IS BLOOD RED?
by Shirley
Without a microscope, blood looks red because there are so many red blood cells in it!
In every drop of blood there are millions of red blood cells.

Now we were in the blood,
but it did not look red.
"Blood is not just a red liquid,"
explained Ms. Frizzle.
"Blood is made of cells,
floating in a clear fluid."
"Those cells look like red rubber saucers!"
someone called out.
"Those are red blood cells," Ms. Frizzle said.
"Red blood cells carry oxygen from the lungs
to all the cells of the body."

DID YOU SEE THAT?

RED BLOOD CELLS CARRY OXYGEN

FOOD MOLECULES

1   2

WHITE BLOOD CELLS

Here and there a white blood cell was busy destroying disease germs. "White blood cells are like soldiers protecting your body from enemies," said Ms. Frizzle.

THE WHITE BLOOD CELL **ATE** THE GERM.

THAT'S DISGUSTING!

WHAT IS BLOOD FOR?
by Ralph
Your blood is like a delivery service. It carries food and oxygen to your body's cells and waste products away from the cells.

PLATELETS
(HELP STOP BLEEDING WHEN YOU GET A CUT)

RALPH'S DELIVERY

FOOD

3   4

DESTROY DISEASE GERMS

DISEASE GERMS

17

Looking back, we saw a white blood cell
chasing the bus.
"We'll be safer with the red blood cells, kids,"
said Ms. Frizzle.
She reached for the handle
that controlled the bus's doors.
"Don't do it!" we cried,
but when did Ms. Frizzle ever listen?
The doors of the bus flew open.

THAT WHITE BLOOD
CELL MUST THINK
THE SCHOOL BUS
IS A GERM.

WELL, THE BUS
IS PRETTY DIRTY.

We were swept out of the bus
and into the bloodstream.
"Everybody hitch a ride!" called The Friz.
Each kid grabbed a red blood cell
as it went by.
Our last glimpse of the bus
was when it went into another blood vessel—
with the white blood cell right behind it!

19

YOUR HEART IS A PUMP
by Florrie

When the walls of the heart chambers squeeze together they pump out blood, just the way you can squeeze water out of a plastic squeeze bottle.

OOPS!

HEY!

Right Lung

Left Lung

Heart

YOUR HEART PUMPS USED BLOOD INTO THE LUNGS TO GET FRESH OXYGEN.

RIGHT LUNG

The next thing we knew, we had flowed into the heart. "Inside the heart are four hollow spaces, called *chambers*," said Ms. F. "Each chamber is a little pump." The two chambers on the right side of the heart took in used blood from the body and pumped it to the lungs.

TO THE RIGHT LUNG

USED BLOOD FROM UPPER BODY

1st CHAMBER

HAVE A HEART, MS. FRIZZLE, GET US OUT OF HERE!

USED BLOOD FROM LOWER BODY

2nd CHAMBER

BLOOD GOES ROUND
AND ROUND
      by Michael
In less than a minute
your blood makes
a trip all around
your body.
    This is called the
circulation of the
blood.

ONE MORE SCIENCE WORD
      by Dorothy Ann
Circulate comes from
a word that means
"to circle". Blood
circulates - circles -
all around your body.

From the lungs, our red blood cells
carried us back to the heart.
This time we were on the left side
of the heart—the side that pumps
fresh blood back to the body again.
"Kids, it looks as if these red
blood cells are on their way to
the brain," said Ms. Frizzle.

LOOK! WHEN THE
RED BLOOD CELLS
PICK UP OXYGEN, THEY
TURN BRIGHT RED.

FROM RIGHT LUNG

AIR SAC

22

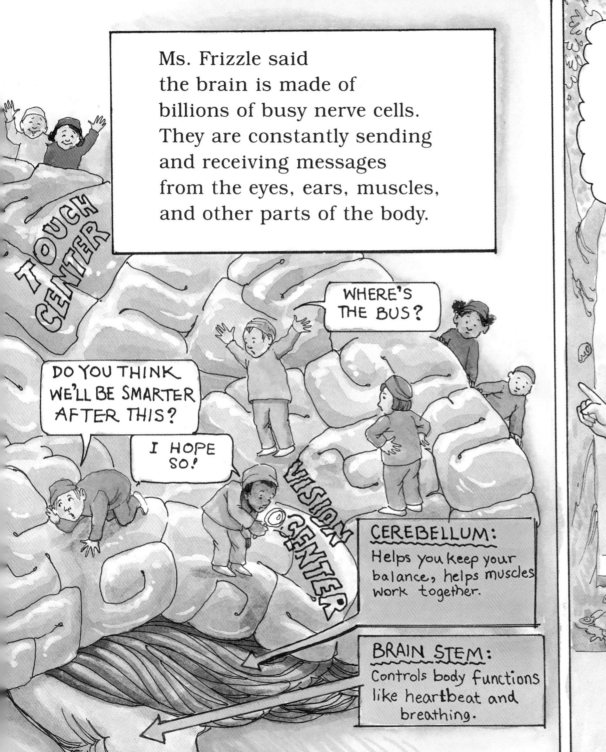

Ms. Frizzle said the brain is made of billions of busy nerve cells. They are constantly sending and receiving messages from the eyes, ears, muscles, and other parts of the body.

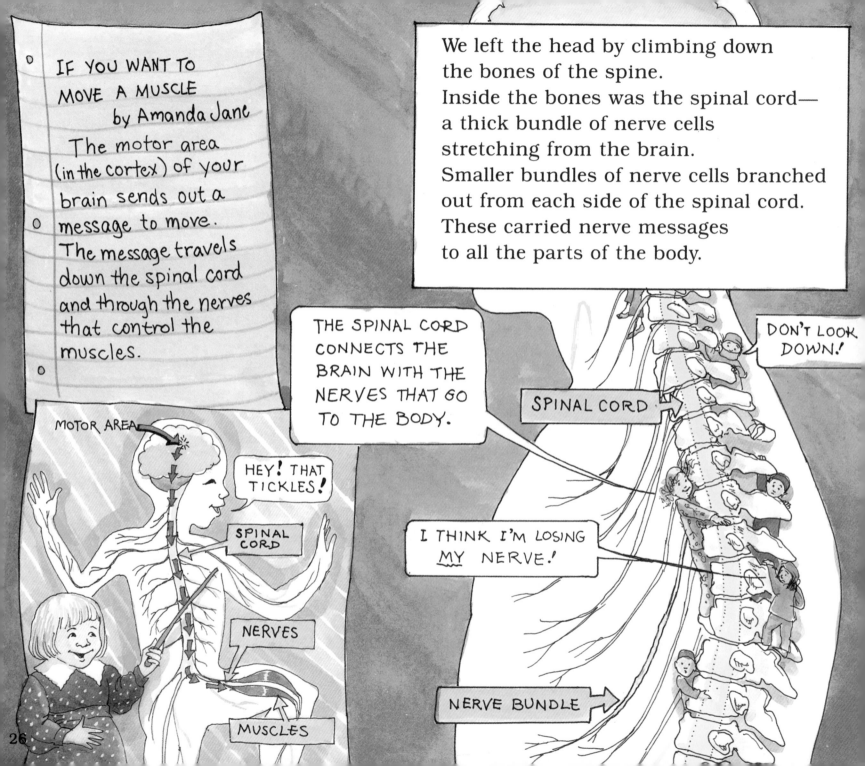

IF YOU WANT TO MOVE A MUSCLE
by Amanda Jane

The motor area (in the cortex) of your brain sends out a message to move. The message travels down the spinal cord and through the nerves that control the muscles.

We left the head by climbing down the bones of the spine.
Inside the bones was the spinal cord— a thick bundle of nerve cells stretching from the brain.
Smaller bundles of nerve cells branched out from each side of the spinal cord.
These carried nerve messages to all the parts of the body.

THE SPINAL CORD CONNECTS THE BRAIN WITH THE NERVES THAT GO TO THE BODY.

DON'T LOOK DOWN!

SPINAL CORD

I THINK I'M LOSING MY NERVE!

MOTOR AREA

HEY! THAT TICKLES!

SPINAL CORD

NERVES

MUSCLES

NERVE BUNDLE

We followed some nerves that went to the leg muscles.
The leg muscles were working hard.
They needed a lot of energy.
They used up a lot of food and oxygen from the blood.
The heart was beating faster to carry fresh blood to the muscle cells.

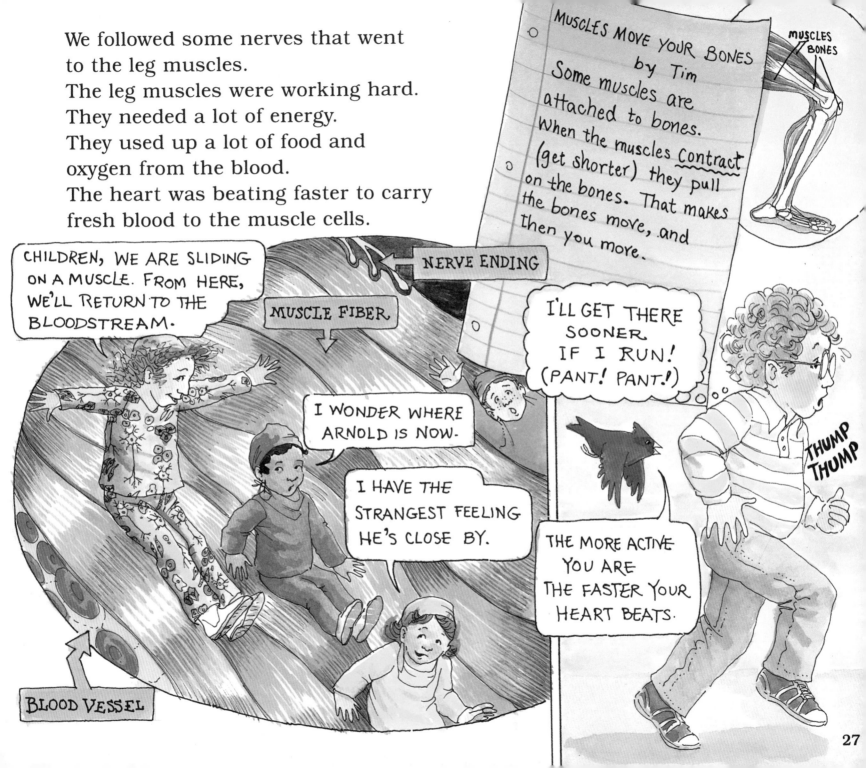

MUSCLES MOVE YOUR BONES
by Tim

Some muscles are attached to bones. When the muscles Contract (get shorter) they pull on the bones. That makes the bones move, and then you more.

MUSCLES
BONES

CHILDREN, WE ARE SLIDING ON A MUSCLE. FROM HERE, WE'LL RETURN TO THE BLOODSTREAM.

NERVE ENDING

MUSCLE FIBER

I'LL GET THERE SOONER IF I RUN! (PANT! PANT!)

I WONDER WHERE ARNOLD IS NOW.

I HAVE THE STRANGEST FEELING HE'S CLOSE BY.

THE MORE ACTIVE YOU ARE THE FASTER YOUR HEART BEATS.

THUMP THUMP

BLOOD VESSEL

We entered a nearby blood vessel.
The blood was moving so fast,
we were afraid we would
lose each other.
But at that moment,
the school bus floated by.
What a relief!
We jumped on and went up
through the heart and lungs again—
just the way we went before.

CLASS, WE'RE ON THE WAY OUT OF THE BODY.

RELAX, WE'RE GOING BACK NOW.

I CAN'T RELAX AS LONG AS I SEE BLOOD CELLS OUTSIDE THE WINDOW.

When we emerged from the bloodsteam,
we were in a huge open space.
"Where are we?" asked a kid.
Ms. Frizzle explained,
"Children, this is the nasal cavity."
"The what?" we asked.
"The inside of the nose," said The Friz.
Suddenly, we heard a deafening noise.
It sounded like "Ah-aa-aa-ah!"

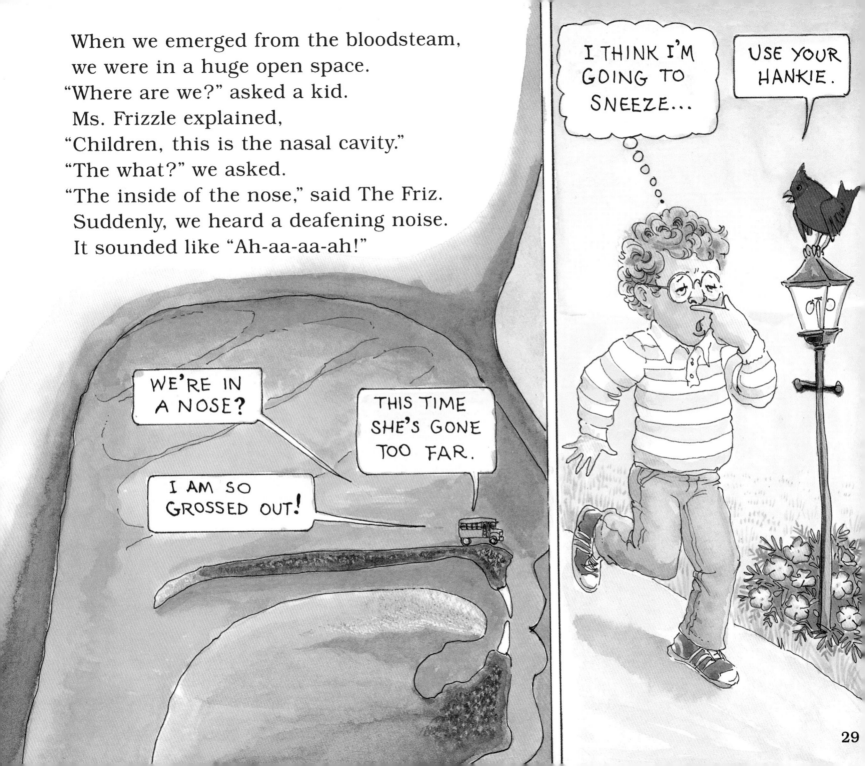

WE'RE IN A NOSE?

I AM SO GROSSED OUT!

THIS TIME SHE'S GONE TOO FAR.

I THINK I'M GOING TO SNEEZE...

USE YOUR HANKIE.

WHAT MAKES YOU SNEEZE?
by Phoebe

If something is tickling the inside of your nose, the tickling signals your brain.

The brain makes you take an extra big breath. (That's when you say Aaah!)

Then your brain makes your chest muscles squeeze your lungs.

Air rushes out at speeds of up to 100 miles per hour. (Thats when you say choo!)

Then we heard, "CHOOOOOO!"

CLASS, THE SOUND YOU HEAR IS A SNEEZE.

ANYTHING IN THE NOSE CAN MAKE YOU SNEEZE. IT COULD BE A BIT OF DIRT OR DUST, OR SOME BACTERIA.

IN THIS CASE IT HAPPENS TO BE A SCHOOL BUS.

A tremendous blast of air
hit the bus full force.
We flew forward,
spinning around and around.

CHILDREN, PREPARE
FOR LANDING.
PLEASE REMAIN SEATED
UNTIL THE SCHOOL BUS
HAS COME TO A
COMPLETE STOP.

IS SHE FOR REAL?

A-A-A-AH
CHOO!

GESUNDHEIT!

31

We were going so fast,
we couldn't see anything,
but we could tell we were getting bigger.
Then—thud!—we landed.
There we were, back at school.
And there was Arnold,
in the school parking lot,
blowing his nose.

WE'RE BACK!

LOOK! THERE'S ARNOLD!

THUD

"Arnold!" we said, "the trip was *amazing!*
You should have been there!"

WHERE WERE YOU?

Back in the classroom,
it was business as usual.
Ms. Frizzle made us draw
a chart of the human body
for the bulletin board.

THE KIDNEYS CLEAN YOUR BLOOD AND MAKE URINE.

THE BLADDER STORES URINE.

KIDNEYS

BLADDER

LIVER

STOMACH

THE LIVER STORES VITAMINS AND DESTROYS POISONS. IT ALSO MAKES BILE, A FLUID THAT HELPS DIGEST FATTY FOODS.

NERVE

BLOOD VESSEL

BONE

MUSCLE

TRUE-OR-FALSE TEST

STOP! TAKE THIS TEST!
DO NOT WATCH T.V. ... YET.
DO NOT GET A SNACK ... YET.
DO NOT PLAY A VIDEO
GAME ... YET.

FIRST TAKE THIS TEST.

HOW TO:
Read the sentences below. Decide if each one is true or false. To see if you are correct, check the answers on the opposite page.

QUESTIONS:

1. A school bus can enter someone's body and kids can go on a tour. True or false?

2. Museums are boring. True or false?

3. Arnold should not have tried to get back to school by himself. True or false?

4. Children cannot breathe or talk when they are surrounded by a liquid. True or false?

5. If the children really were as small as cells, we couldn't see them without a microscope. True or false?

6. White blood cells actually chase and destroy disease germs. True or false?

7. Ms. Frizzle really knew where Arnold was the whole time. True or false?

ANSWERS:

1. False! That could not happen in real life. (Not even to Arnold.)

But in this story the author had to make it happen. Otherwise, the book would have been about a trip to a museum, instead of a trip through the body.

2. False! Museums are interesting and fun. But they are not as weird and gross as actually going inside a human body.

3. True! In real life, it would have been safer if Arnold had found a police officer to help.

4. True! If children were *really* inside a blood vessel, they would drown. It must have been magic.

5. True! The pictures in this book show the cells and the children greatly enlarged.

6. True! As unbelievable as it seems, real white blood cells actually behave just like the ones in this book. They even squeeze through the cells of blood vessel walls to capture germs in your organs and tissues.

7. Probably true. No one is absolutely sure, but most people think Ms. Frizzle knows *everything*.

PLEASE DO NOT WRITE IN THIS BOOK.

THANK YOU.